# Flowchart Smart

# The Science of the

# SENSES

Richard and Louise Spilsbury

**Gareth Stevens**
PUBLISHING

Please visit our website, **www.garethstevens.com**.
For a free color catalog of all our high-quality books,
call toll free 1-800-542-2595 of fax 1-877-542-2596.

Cataloging-in-Publication Data

Names: Spilsbury, Richard.
Title: The science of the senses / Richard and Louise Spilsbury.
Description: New York : Gareth Stevens Publishing, 2018. | Series: Flowchart smart | Includes index.
Identifiers: ISBN 9781538207000 (pbk.) | ISBN 9781538206959 (library bound) | ISBN 9781538206850 (6 pack)
Subjects: LCSH: Senses and sensation--Juvenile literature.
Classification: LCC QP434.S65 2018 | DDC 612.8--dc23

First Edition

Published in 2018 by
**Gareth Stevens Publishing**
111 East 14th Street, Suite 349
New York, NY 10003

Copyright © 2018 Gareth Stevens Publishing

Produced for Gareth Stevens by Calcium
Editors: Sarah Eason and Harriet McGregor
Designers: Paul Myerscough and Simon Borrough
Picture researcher: Rachel Blount

Cover art: Shutterstock: Nikiteev Konstantin.

Picture credits: Shutterstock: Alliance 34–35, Andrey_Popov 44, Billion Photos 20, Blambca 9, Samuel Borges Photography 10b, Connel 7t, Denk Creative 30, 39, Dragon_fang 40b, Dwphotos 18–19, Espies 44–45, Lukas Gojda 14–15, Tom Gowanlock 1, 32–33, Holbox 36–37, Inu 28–29, KonstantinChristian 26–27, Kzenon 22–23, LHF Graphics 24, Venturelli Luca 6–7, Manzrussali 4–5, Maridav 28b, Volodymyr Martyniuk 10–11, Alexander Mazurkevich 4b, Rafal Olechowski 40–41, Anna Om 12–13, Photobank Gallery 12b, Andy Piatt 34l, Peter Polak 21, Sianstock 26b, Stockphoto Mania 19t, Subidubi 17, 43, Viktor1 36b, Wavebreakmedia 14b, 32b.

Printed in the United States of America
CPSIA compliance information: Batch #CS17GS: For further information contact Gareth Stevens, New York, New York at 1-800-542-2595.

# Contents

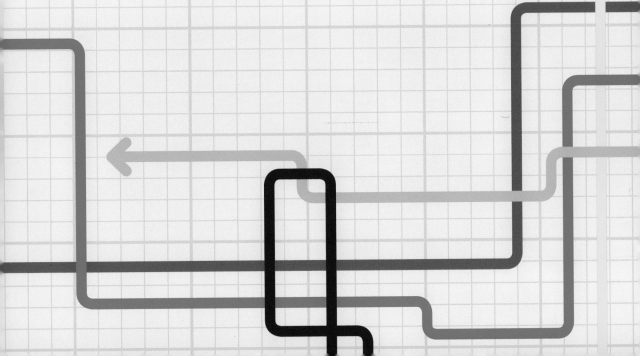

# Chapter 1

# It Makes Sense!

Think about what happens at a firework display. You hear loud bangs and screaming whistles of firecrackers and rockets in the air. You see brightly colored patterns of light in the dark sky and smell the smoke. You feel the heat from a bonfire warm your skin and you taste the hot dogs. You can do all of these things thanks to your senses!

Senses are essential to our lives. They allow us to enjoy and understand the world around us. There are five main ways we use our senses: we see with our eyes, touch with our skin, smell with our nose, taste with our tongue, and hear with our ears. Our senses often work together and some senses do more than one job at a time. For example, we taste food using both our sense of taste and our sense of smell.

People are tempted to buy spices here by their smell, taste, and glorious colors.

Senses are a collection of **sensory organs** or **cells** in the human body that respond to particular sensations outside the body. The senses collect information about these sensations. They send the information to the brain along pathways called **nerves**. The brain figures out what these signals mean and then decides how your body should react to the sensation.

People experience firework displays with all of their senses.

## Get Smart!

Some people do not have the use of all their senses. For example, if someone cannot see, they are blind, or if they cannot hear, they are deaf. However, if one sense stops working, the other senses may take over or become stronger to make up for the missing sense.

# Senses and Safety

One of the most important reasons for having senses is to keep safe. Senses provide people with information about how their bodies are affected by the world around them. As well as helping them work, play, and communicate, senses also help them escape danger.

Senses are the human body's early warning system. Sound travels over long distances. Loud noise-making devices such as emergency sirens can alert a whole town of people and warn them about a threat long before it is close enough for them to be endangered by it. Police, ambulances, and other safety vehicles rely on alerting people's senses using sirens and flashing lights. They give a clear signal to traffic and walkers to allow them to pass.

## Get Smart!

Skin can sense touch, temperature, and pain. Pain is a very important sensation. It is the body's way of keeping safe. Imagine if you spilled boiling water on your hand. You would feel pain that told you to move your hand away from the water as fast as possible. The pain would continue for some time to remind you not to use the hand until it healed.

This ambulance must move quickly through busy streets so it is using its siren and flashing lights to warn people to keep out of the way.

To keep safe and ensure the body is ready to respond to an emergency, the senses usually only tell the brain about new and important things. Even though people may not be aware of it, their senses and brain are constantly assessing their surroundings and filtering out a lot of background information that they do not need to think about. The senses usually tell the brain about its surroundings only when they change. So someone would not notice the feeling of shoes on their feet until they get wet and their senses tell the brain they are standing in a puddle!

Cyclists do not wear earphones while they are on the road so they can hear traffic coming toward them.

Get flowchart smart!

# Keeping Safe

Follow the flowchart to see how people's senses alert them to danger.

There is a fire in an office building.

The sound of a fire alarm alerts the office workers to the danger.

Together their senses ensure they have all the information they need to get to safety, fast.

Their skin detects a change in temperature, so they can feel how close the threat is and be sure they move away from the fire.

Flowchart Smart

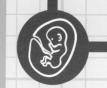

Their noses smell *the* smoke from the fire.

As *they* breathe, *they* can even taste *the* smoke in *the* air.

Their eyes see *the* smoke and other people running *to* leave *the* building and escape danger.

# Chapter 2
# Sight

Our eyes give us our all-important sense of sight but we can only see because of light. We see when light **reflects**, or bounces, off an object and enters our eyes. That is why we cannot use our sense of sight when it is completely dark.

Things that give off light, such as the sun, lamps, and cell phone screens, are **luminous**. The sun is our most important natural source of light. During the day people see objects when light from the sun reflects off them into the eyes. When it is dark, light from flashlights, lamps, and other luminous objects reflects off surfaces so people can see them.

In both a human eye and a camera, light passes through a **lens** and forms an image.

Light is a form of energy. It travels from its source in straight lines until it hits another object. When it hits an object, light is either **absorbed** or reflected. When light reflects, it bounces off a surface a little like a ball bounces off a wall. When it reflects toward us, it enters our eyes and helps us see.

Strong sunlight can damage eyes, so it is important to wear wide-brimmed hats and sunglasses on sunny days. People also wear goggles to protect their eyes when playing sports such as squash. Staring at a computer screen for long periods of time makes eyes dry and tired, so it is important to take regular breaks and look out of the window to give the eyes a change of view. People should also have their eyes checked regularly by an optician.

People have two eyes to help them judge distance and figure out how far away something is.

## Get Smart!

Have you ever wondered why we have two eyes instead of one? The brain uses the images passed to it from both eyes to help people see in three dimensions (3-D) and judge distances.

# Inside the Eye

The human eye works a little like a camera. A lens at the front collects light and **focuses** it on a **sensitive** area inside. This area interprets the signals and turns them into images!

Light enters the human eye through the **pupil**. The pupil is the tiny black hole in the middle of the iris (the colored part of the eye). It passes through a curved part called a lens, which changes shape to help it focus light onto the **retina** clearly. The retina is the surface at the back of the eyeball. It is covered with two types of light sensitive cells: cones and rods. The rods are most sensitive to light and dark changes, shape, and movement. The cones allow people to see color.

The retina sends signals about what the eyes see to the brain along the **optic nerve**. The image that the retina receives from the lens is upside down and backward. The brain interprets the signals and turns the image the right way up so we know what we are looking at.

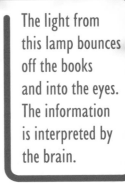

The light from this lamp bounces off the books and into the eyes. The information is interpreted by the brain.

When people are awake, their eyes are constantly working to control how much light gets into them and to focus on different things. The iris is a circle of muscle that can change the size of the pupil. In low light, eyes need to take in more light to be able to see clearly, so the iris muscles make the pupil bigger. In bright light, the iris muscles make the pupil smaller to prevent eye damage. Other eye muscles change the shape of the lens to allow it to focus on objects at different distances.

There are about 120 million rods and between six and seven million cones in the human retina, which collect data about what the eyes see.

# How Glasses Work

The eyes must focus light accurately on the retina for people to see perfectly. If the lenses in a person's eyes do not bend light onto the retina properly, they may need to wear glasses to help them see more clearly.

When someone is shortsighted they cannot clearly see distant objects. Their lenses focus the image a little in front of the retina, instead of directly onto it. People who are farsighted can see distant objects clearly, but close objects look blurry. Their lenses focus the image behind the retina instead of directly onto it. The plastic lenses in glasses are curved to make them **refract**, or bend, light so that it hits the retina properly again.

Light travels at different speeds through different substances. It moves faster through air than water. A straw in a glass of water looks bent or broken from the side because light slows down when it moves into the water from the air. As light slows down it bends. This is refraction. Light also refracts when it shines into transparent glass or plastic. People who are shortsighted wear **concave** lenses that bend light outward to help the lenses in their eyes focus light on the retina. People who are farsighted have glasses with **convex** lenses that bend light inward to help their lenses focus light on their retina.

Opticians check people's eyesight to find out if they are short- or farsighted.

14

Contact lenses are curved lenses that refract light to help people see. They are worn directly on the surface of the eye. Contact lenses are made from thin, soft, and flexible plastic and cover the iris. Liquid on the surface of the eyes helps hold them in place.

The contact lens is held on the tip of a finger before being placed on the eye.

Get flowchart smart!

# How Eyes Work

Use this flowchart to find out how eyes let us see.

Light enters the human eye through the pupil, the tiny black hole in the middle of the iris.

The lens changes shape to refract the **rays** of light and focus them directly onto the retina.

The brain interprets the signals and turns the image the right way up so we know what we are looking at.

The cone cells in the retina interpret the colors in what you see and the rods in the retina sense light and dark changes, shape, and movement.

The retina sends this information in the form of electrical signals along the optic nerve to the brain.

Flowchart Smart

# Chapter 3
# Hearing

We live in a world of sound. It is rare that we experience silence. Even when we are alone there is the sound of our own breathing. Sounds help us communicate, give us information, warn us of danger, and give us pleasure.

There are many different sounds in the world, but they are all made by **vibrations**. When something vibrates, it moves up and down or back and forth very quickly, again and again. When someone plucks a guitar string or taps the skin of a drum we can actually see these vibrations. When we speak or sing, vocal cords inside our throat vibrate. Sound vibrations, or **sound waves**, spread out in the air all around the source of the sound. When they reach a human ear, the ear collects the sound waves. It converts the sound waves to signals that are sent to the brain so it can figure out what the sounds are.

Listening to our favorite music is just one of the ways our sense of hearing helps us.

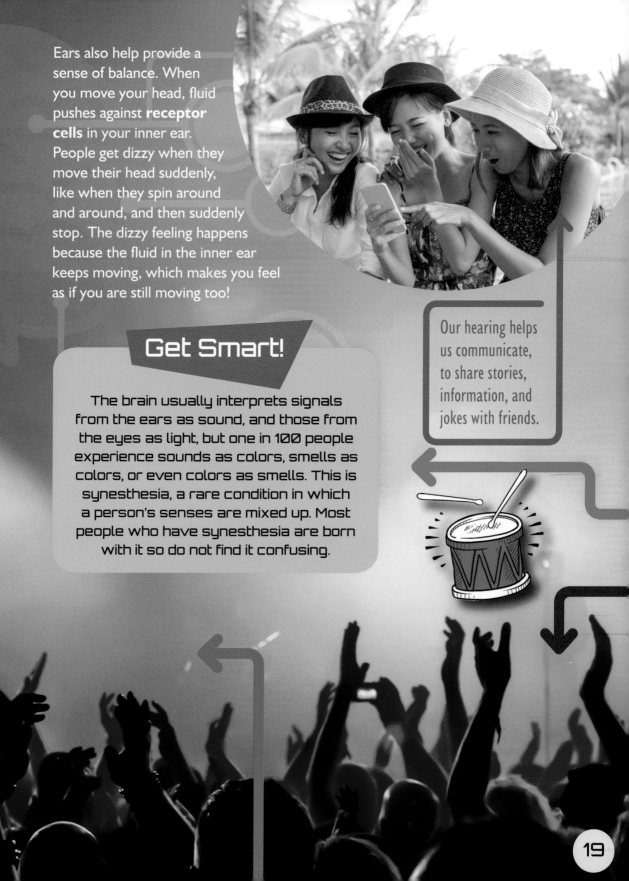

Ears also help provide a sense of balance. When you move your head, fluid pushes against **receptor cells** in your inner ear. People get dizzy when they move their head suddenly, like when they spin around and around, and then suddenly stop. The dizzy feeling happens because the fluid in the inner ear keeps moving, which makes you feel as if you are still moving too!

## Get Smart!

The brain usually interprets signals from the ears as sound, and those from the eyes as light, but one in 100 people experience sounds as colors, smells as colors, or even colors as smells. This is synesthesia, a rare condition in which a person's senses are mixed up. Most people who have synesthesia are born with it so do not find it confusing.

Our hearing helps us communicate, to share stories, information, and jokes with friends.

# How Ears Work

The earflaps on the outside of a human head have an important job. They collect the vibrations made by sounds in the air. The outer part of the ear funnels the sound waves inside the ear so we can hear them.

When we cup our hand around our ear we help channel more sound waves into the inner ear.

Inside the ear, the sound waves travel through a short tunnel called the ear canal until they hit a thin sheet of skin called the eardrum. The sound waves make the eardrum vibrate, a little like the skin of a real drum. The vibrations move in a similar way to the original source of the vibration. The eardrum passes the vibrations through three tiny bones called **ossicles** into the inner part of the ear. The ossicles increase the vibrations and pass them into a tube called the **cochlea**.

The cochlea is a snail-shaped tube that contains liquid and 30,000 tiny nerves called hair cells, which look like very tiny hairs. The vibrations move the hair cells and the hair cells change the vibrations into electrical signals. Each hair cell receives and codes different sounds. The signals are sent to the brain through the **auditory** (hearing) nerve. In an instant, the brain interprets the signals and tells you what the sounds are.

When someone shouts they create large vibrations, or sound waves, in the air around their mouths.

## Get Smart!

There is a very good reason that we have two ears instead of one. The ear closest to the sound hears it a split second earlier and a little more loudly than the other ear. The brain uses this slight difference to figure out which direction the sound is coming from.

# Loud and Soft

Humans can hear a whole range of different sounds. Some sounds are loud like a train thundering past or music blaring from a giant loudspeaker at a concert. Some sounds are quiet, like the sound of someone gently breathing or leaves rustling in the wind. Sounds are loud or quiet depending on the energy in the vibrations.

Things make more noise the more they vibrate. The harder a drum or door is struck, the bigger and stronger the vibrations, and the louder the sounds. A guitar string plucked gently or fingers lightly tapped on a surface make smaller vibrations and quieter sounds. The amount of energy put in to create the vibrations gives the sounds more or less energy too.

Another thing that affects the **volume**, or loudness, of a sound is distance. The farther away you are from a sound, the quieter it becomes. Imagine a friend shouts to you across a great distance. The sounds they make use energy to push the air in front of them as they move. As they use up energy, the sound vibrations get smaller and the sounds grow quieter until the energy is used up and the sounds stop.

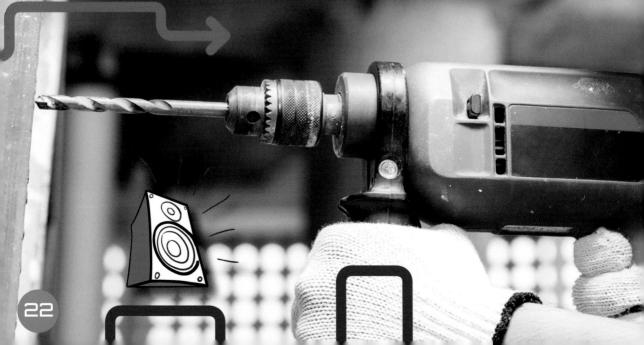

People who work with noisy equipment, tools, or vehicles wear earmuffs to protect their sense of hearing.

## Get Smart!

Volume is measured in units called decibels. One decibel is the smallest sound we can hear and a jet airplane taking off is about 120 decibels (dB). Sounds louder than 85 dB can cause vibrations that bend or break the hair cells in the cochlea, especially if they continue for a long time. It is best to avoid having the volume high on earphones or speakers.

Get flowchart smart!

# How Ears Hear Sounds

Take a look at this flowchart to understand how we hear sounds.

A drum is struck, the drum skin vibrates, and the vibrations create sound waves in the air.

The outer parts of the ear collect some of these sound waves and funnel them into the ear.

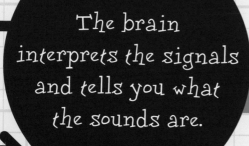

The brain interprets the signals and tells you what the sounds are.

The sound waves travel through the ear canal and hit the eardrum, making it vibrate.

The eardrum passes the vibrations to three tiny bones called ossicles, which increase the vibrations and pass them into the cochlea.

The vibrations move hair cells in the cochlea. They change the vibrations into electrical signals and send them through the auditory nerve to the brain.

Flowchart Smart

# Chapter 4
# Touch

Skin gives people their sense of touch and the ability to feel **pressure**, pain, heat, and cold. We can instantly feel the difference between smooth metal and rough surfaces like sand. We can sense the chill of ice in our mouth or the warmth and weight of a cup full of hot chocolate when we hold it in our hands.

People can feel many different levels of pressure, too, from the gentle feeling of a cat's fur as it brushes against the skin, to the stronger pushing force of a heavy weight on the lap. The reason the human body can sense such a variety of different feelings is that the skin, mouth, and tongue contain millions of different specialized touch receptors.

When someone touches an object, touch receptors help the brain understand what they are touching and how it is affecting them. Nerves carry information collected by the receptors to the sensory area of the brain. This area of the brain analyzes and processes everything felt through the skin, mouth, and tongue. It decides whether it is safe to go on touching the object or whether the person should withdraw from it immediately.

Braille is a form of written language for people who cannot see. It is read using the sense of touch.

## Get Smart!

Pain warns people of danger and keeps them from repeating any actions that cause pain, such as touching something that is too hot. Some people are born with a rare condition that means they cannot feel pain. This is very dangerous because without a feeling of pain people do not realize when they have hurt themselves.

A newborn baby's sense of touch is very important. Being held and stroked by parents gives them a sense of security, love, and comfort.

# Getting Under the Skin

Human skin is so sensitive and can identify so many different kinds of touch and pressure because it has millions of touch receptors beneath its surface. They are divided into six different types. Some are located near the surface of the skin and some are much deeper below the skin's surface.

The first three types of receptors are free nerve endings, hair follicle receptors, and Meissner corpuscles. They respond to light touches and are all located at or near the surface of the skin. Free nerve endings are found at the surface of the skin and they are sensitive to pain, temperature change, and itchiness. Hair follicle receptors are located in hair follicles, the cells that surround the root of a hair, and sense any position changes of the hair strands. Meissner corpuscles detect changes in texture.

Free nerve endings in the hands tell us when we are holding something cold like ice and tell us when that begins to hurt!

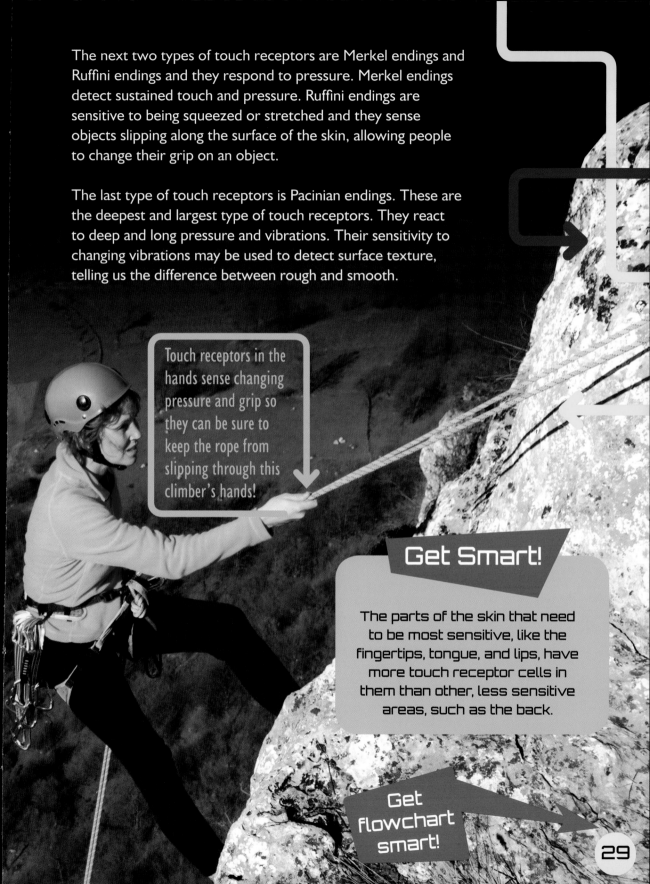

The next two types of touch receptors are Merkel endings and Ruffini endings and they respond to pressure. Merkel endings detect sustained touch and pressure. Ruffini endings are sensitive to being squeezed or stretched and they sense objects slipping along the surface of the skin, allowing people to change their grip on an object.

The last type of touch receptors is Pacinian endings. These are the deepest and largest type of touch receptors. They react to deep and long pressure and vibrations. Their sensitivity to changing vibrations may be used to detect surface texture, telling us the difference between rough and smooth.

Touch receptors in the hands sense changing pressure and grip so they can be sure to keep the rope from slipping through this climber's hands!

## Get Smart!

The parts of the skin that need to be most sensitive, like the fingertips, tongue, and lips, have more touch receptor cells in them than other, less sensitive areas, such as the back.

Get flowchart smart!

# How Touch Works

This flowchart takes us through the steps that make our sense of touch work.

When you touch something, touch receptors in the skin sense it.

The sensory area of the brain analyzes and processes the information to decide if it is safe to go on touching the object or whether you should move away from it immediately.

Different touch receptors respond to different aspects of the sensations. Some touch receptors identify if it is hot or cold and others figure out what kind of pressure it is exerting.

The touch receptors code the information they collect and send it along nerves to the sensory area of the brain.

Flowchart Smart

# Chapter 5
# Taste

The tongue and brain are used to give us our sense of taste. The nose plays an important part too. In fact, when we taste food, around 75 percent of what we think is taste is actually smell! Our sense of taste can detect different flavors in food and drink that help us identify and enjoy food. It can also tell us when something is rotten so we stop eating it.

The sense of taste works by responding to molecules released from our food and drink when we chew or **digest** them. A molecule is the smallest possible amount of a substance. The receptor cells that detect taste are found in taste buds on the surface of the tongue. They react to the tiny molecules and send taste information to nearby nerves, which send messages to the brain.

Freshly baked cookies smell delicious, but try holding your nose closed while eating one. Because smell and taste are so closely linked you will not get the full flavor of the food if you cannot smell it.

When someone is hungry, their sense of smell increases. When they bite into and chew food, the food releases molecules that travel up the throat and into the nose. The molecules trigger receptors inside the nose. These work together with taste buds on the tongue to tell the brain all about the full flavor of the food that is being eaten. After eating, the increased smell sensitivity goes back to normal again. This also explains why food does not taste as good when we have a cold and a stuffy nose.

## Get Smart!

Some animals have taste receptors in places other than their tongue or mouth. Flies and butterflies, for example, have taste receptors on their feet, so they can taste anything they land on. A catfish has taste receptors across its entire body.

Our sense of taste tells us that ice cream is sweet. Our sense of taste also protects us against eating harmful substances. For example, poisonous plants often taste bitter, which makes us spit out the plant.

# How Do Taste Buds Work?

If you stick out your tongue and look at it in a mirror, you should see a lot of small lumps over its surface. These little lumps are papillae, and most of them contain taste buds, which help give us our sense of taste.

Taste buds are found on the tongue, the roof of the mouth, and the lining of the throat. Each taste bud contains about 100 taste receptor cells. Before taste buds can get to work, the mouth must begin to break down the foods in the mouth. It is not possible to taste things in the mouth if the **saliva**, or spit, cannot **dissolve** them. After saliva dissolves the food, the receptors on the taste buds can detect molecules within the food. If the tongue is completely dry, it is almost impossible to taste dry, salty, or sugary foods.

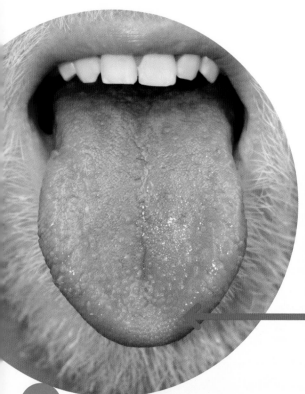

Children have taste buds spread throughout their mouths. Adults have one-third the number of taste buds and they are mostly on the tongue.

The papillae on the top of the tongue not only contain the taste buds, they also help grip food while we are chewing it.

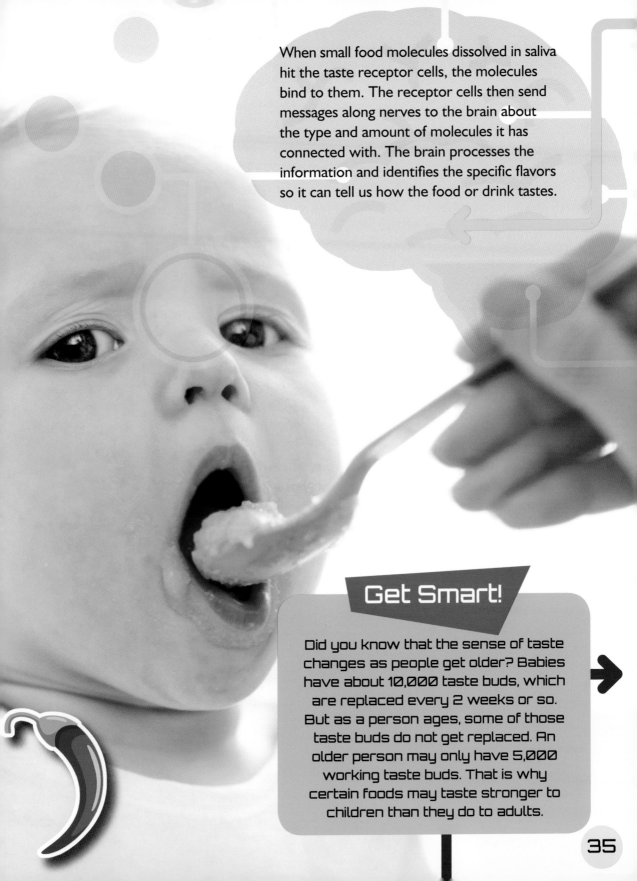

When small food molecules dissolved in saliva hit the taste receptor cells, the molecules bind to them. The receptor cells then send messages along nerves to the brain about the type and amount of molecules it has connected with. The brain processes the information and identifies the specific flavors so it can tell us how the food or drink tastes.

## Get Smart!

Did you know that the sense of taste changes as people get older? Babies have about 10,000 taste buds, which are replaced every 2 weeks or so. But as a person ages, some of those taste buds do not get replaced. An older person may only have 5,000 working taste buds. That is why certain foods may taste stronger to children than they do to adults.

# Different Tastes

Traditionally, tastes are grouped into four basic types: salt, sweet, bitter, and sour. Each of the several thousand taste buds on the tongue can recognize any of the tastes. Then it is up to the brain to figure out which is which.

Being able to detect different tastes does not only make food more interesting, it is what makes us hungry and it also protects us from poisons. The reason the human body likes the taste of sugar is because it needs **carbohydrates**, which are sugars, for energy. The body likes salty flavors because the body needs salt to maintain fluid balance, allow muscles to relax, and nerves to transmit signals. Salt also helps keep a normal **blood pressure**. The reason we do not like most bitter and sour flavors is that most bitter substances are bad for you and food that turns sour is usually rotten!

Since 2002, a fifth taste has been added to the list: umami. Umami is not sweet, bitter, sour, salty, or any combination of those four tastes. It is the deep, dark, meaty flavor found in foods such as chicken broth, soy sauce, anchovies, and mushrooms. A Japanese scientist named Kikunae Ikeda identified the taste as coming from glutamic acid. He called it "umami," which means "delicious" in Japanese.

We can detect different tastes at the same time, such as a sharp or sour raspberry, bitter mint, and sweet ice cream.

Many restaurants use a small amount of chopped anchovies to give food a savory umami flavor.

## Get Smart!

Most people do not like really bitter tastes, but some people build up a liking for certain bitter flavors as they get older. For example, adults often enjoy the bitter taste of coffee. They may also enjoy the taste of capsaicin, the substance in chili peppers that makes them hot and triggers heat and pain receptor cells. This taste makes curries and Mexican foods popular.

Get flowchart smart!

# How Taste Works

Follow the flowchart to understand the sense of taste.

When people chew food, saliva helps dissolve it and release tiny molecules of the food.

Some of these molecules travel up the throat and into the nose. **Olfactory** receptors send information to the brain about how the food smells to help the brain identify its flavor.

The brain processes the information from the nose and the tongue to identify the specific flavor of the food.

Some of the molecules land on taste receptor cells on taste buds on the tongue, the roof of the mouth, and the throat.

The food molecules bind to the taste receptor cells, which send information about the molecules along nerves to the brain.

Flowchart Smart

# Chapter 6
# Smell

Did you know that even while you were a baby developing inside your mother, you had a sense of smell? The sense of smell is the first of all the senses to develop and even before you are born, it is fully formed and working.

As humans grow up, they learn to identify different smells so that their brains remember smells and they can recognize them instantly. That is how people know something in the kitchen is burning as soon as they smell smoke or that a glass of juice is orange or apple flavored before they taste or see it. Smells provide information about the surroundings and keep people safe. For example, the sense of smell can warn someone not to eat something that smells rotten.

The sense of smell gets bored easily. This is called olfactory fatigue and it is designed to keep people safe. When someone goes into a bakery, the smell of fresh bread seems to be very strong. But after a few minutes, the different scents of baking become less obvious. The sense of smell blocks scents after it has identified them as not being a threat so that it is free to check for new smells that might cause trouble.

The smell of sour milk is very distinctive. We know not to drink it.

The sense of smell is closely linked to memory. People can only remember things they have seen with about 50 percent accuracy after 3 months. But they can usually remember smells with 65 percent accuracy after a year! That is because the part of the brain responsible for smell is linked to parts that are responsible for memory, learning, and emotions too.

Smell and memory are connected. As adults, people are more likely to remember things they smell as children than things they hear or even see!

Get flowchart smart!

# How the Nose Works

Follow the steps in this flowchart to understand how the nose senses odors.

When someone sucks air in through their nostrils to smell roses, odor molecules from the roses are carried with the air up the nose.

The air carrying the odor molecules enters the **nasal cavity**, where they hit the **olfactory epithelium**, or smelling skin.

The brain decodes and interprets the combination of the signals it receives from the receptor cells to identify different smells.

Some odor molecules are trapped by hairlike endings called **cilia**. These are found on receptor cells in the olfactory epithelium.

The receptor cells send signals along the olfactory nerve to the brain.

Flowchart Smart

# Inside the Nose

Compared with other animals, humans have a weak sense of smell but we can still smell about 10,000 different odors!

Everything you smell, from freshly cut grass to a pizza baking in an open oven, gives off molecules. Odor molecules are generally light, so they float easily through the air into your nose. When someone sucks air in through the nostrils to smell something, it goes up the nose and into the nasal cavity, a space behind the nose. The roof of the nasal cavity is the olfactory epithelium. This is a very thin layer of skin that is lined with receptor cells.

Your nose is at work all day, interpreting different scents, but when you are asleep, your sense of smell shuts down.

There are hundreds of millions of receptor cells in the olfactory epithelium. Each one has hairlike endings called cilia that increase their **surface area**. These are sensitive to odor molecules floating in the air sucked in through a nose. When an odor molecule comes into contact with the receptor cells, the cells send signals along the olfactory nerve to the brain. Then the brain decodes and interprets the combination of all the signals it receives to identify different smells.

Without the brain none of the senses would work. As well as receiving information from the nose, the brain can interpret messages from the eyes, ears, skin, and mouth. It tells you what your senses are receiving from the world and how to respond. Your brain and senses make sense of the world around you!

Our senses of smell, sight, taste, touch, and hearing are on duty every minute we are awake, telling us all we need to know about our surroundings.

## Get Smart!

Did you know that every 4 weeks you get a new nose? Your sense of smell is so important that each one of the hundreds of different receptors in your nose is replaced every 28 days!

# Glossary

**absorbed** Soaked up.

**auditory** Having something to do with hearing.

**blood pressure** The force that the heart uses to pump blood around the body.

**carbohydrates** Substances in foods that give the body energy to live and grow.

**cells** Very small parts that together form all living things.

**cilia** Tiny hairlike part.

**cochlea** A snail-shaped tube in the ear.

**concave** Curving in toward the center.

**convex** Curving outward on each side.

**digest** To break food down so the body can use it.

**dissolve** To break something down in liquid until it becomes part of the liquid.

**focuses** Adjusts to see things clearly.

**lens** The clear part of the eye that focuses light rays on the retina. An artificial lens is a transparent object that refracts (bends) light in useful ways.

**luminous** Gives out light.

**nasal cavity** A space behind the nose.

**nerves** Fibers that carry messages between the brain and the rest of the body.

**olfactory** Having something to do with smell.

**olfactory epithelium** A thin layer that senses smell, also known as the smelling skin.

**optic nerve** A pathway that carries messages from the eye to the brain.

**ossicles** Tiny bones in the inner ear.

**pressure** A pushing force.

**pupil** A tiny opening in the center of the iris that looks black.

**rays** Beams.

**receptor cells** Cells that receive or collect information for the body.

**reflects** Bounces back.

**refract** The way light rays bend when they pass at an angle from one kind of material (such as water) to another (such as air).

**retina** The part at the back of the eye that sends messages about what your eyes see to the brain.

**saliva** Spit.

**sensitive** Having to do with someone who responds easily.

**sensory organs** Groups of receptor cells.

**sound waves** Vibrations that we hear as sound.

**surface area** The total area of the surface of a 3-D object.

**vibrations** Movement back and forth, quickly and repeatedly.

**volume** Loudness of a sound.

# For More Information

## Books

Benbow, Ann and Colin Mably. *Sensational Human Body Science Projects* (Real Life Science Experiments). New York, NY: Enslow Elementary, 2009.

Canavan, Thomas. *Do You Really Taste with Your Nose?* (Human Body FAQ). New York, NY: PowerKids Press, 2017.

Mason, Paul. *Your Mind-Bending Brain and Networking Nervous System* (Your Brilliant Body). New York, NY: Crabtree Publishing Company, 2015.

## Websites

Discover some amazing facts about animal senses at:
**faculty.washington.edu/chudler/amaze.html**

Click on the links on this site to discover more about senses:
**idahoptv.org/sciencetrek/topics/senses/facts.cfm**

Uncover some fascinating facts about how animals sense their surroundings at:
**kids.britannica.com/comptons/article-196394/animal**

Find out more about the five senses at:
**microbemagic.ucc.ie/explore_body/five_senses.html**

# Index